STOPPING BY HOME

OTHER BOOKS BY DAVID HUDDLE:

A Dream With No Stump Roots In It
Paper Boy
Only the Little Bone
The High Spirits: Stories of Men and Women

. . . .

STOPPING
BY HOME

DAVID HUDDLE

Peregrine Smith Books
Salt Lake City

ACKNOWLEDGMENTS

These poems have appeared in *Field, The Little Review, Southern Poetry Review, Longhouse, The Arts Journal, New England Poetry Engagement Book, Mid-American Review, The Agni Review, Ploughshares, Pig Iron, Antietam Review, Virginia Quarterly Review, North by Northeast, Hampden-Sydney Poetry Review, Prairie Schooner.*

"Nerves," "Theory," "Bac Ha," "Words," "Cousin," and "Vermont" appeared in *Carrying the Darkness: American Indochina—The Poetry of the Vietnam War*, W. D. Ehrhart, editor, Avon Books, 1985. "Words" and "Them" appeared in *The Sonnet: An Anthology*, Bender and Squier, editors, Washington Square Press, 1987. "A History of the Pets" appeared in *Pocket Poems*, Paul B. Janeczko, editor, Bradbury Press, 1985. "Stopping by Home" appeared in *Going Over to Your Place: Poems for Each Other*, Paul B. Janeczko, editor, Bradbury Press, 1987.

First edition

92 91 90 89 88   5 4 3 2 1

Published by Gibbs Smith, Publisher, P.O. Box 667, Layton, Utah 84041. This is a Peregrine Smith Book

Design by Smith & Clarkson

Printed and bound in the United States of America

Library of Congress Cataloging-in-Publication Data
Huddle, David, 1942-
    Stopping by home / David Huddle.
        p.   cm.—(Peregrine Smith poetry series : v. 2)
        ISBN 0-87905-521-9 : $9.95
        I. Title. II. Series.
PS3558.U287S7 1988   88-23813
811'.54—dc19   CIP

FOR MY FATHER,
CHARLES R. HUDDLE, JR.,
1911 - 1986

CONTENTS

. . . .

I.
TOUR OF DUTY *1*
Entry *3*
Nerves *3*
Theory *4*
Smoke *4*
Work *5*
New York Laundry *5*
Bac Ha *6*
Haircut *6*
George *7*
Beer *7*
R&R *8*
Revelation *8*
Words *9*
Them *9*
Transfer *10*
Short *10*
Cousin *11*
Vermont *11*

II.
ALBUM *13*
Music *15*
The Field *15*
The House *16*
Two Facts *16*
The Front Yard *17*
Porches *17*
Groceries in the Front Seat *18*
Invention *18*
A History of the Pets *19*
Dr. Zeno's Laboratory *19*
The School *20*
The Air Rifle *20*
Croquet *21*
Icicle *21*
Kitchen Tables *22*
Sunday Dinner *22*
Coda *23*

III.
STOPPING BY HOME *25*

IV.
THINGS I KNOW, THINGS
I DON'T *33*

I.

TOUR OF DUTY

ENTRY

. . . .

Arrived in khakis, overseas cap, bloused boots,
I am standing with a hundred others
like me, new ones in tan at Tan Son Nhut,
crowded around some sergeant whose only words
I will remember are *Welcome to Vietnam.*
Probably he tells us to listen up,
what he has to say may save our lives. I'm
going to hear that a lot. Bad student

as usual I ignore him, gawk at faces,
the wire fence, planes landing, moving light beams.
In this heat, more plant than man, I'm breathing
slowly, registering these queer noises,
noticing all around me M-16s
slung like toys on the backs of the ones in green.

NERVES

Training I received did not apply
because Cu Chi District was not Fort Jackson.
Funniest thing, they had dogs like any-
where, used them for sandwich meat, I ate one
once, but I guess you want to know if I
ever shot somebody—didn't—would have—
curious about it, but my job gave
one duty, to ask questions. I'd lie

if I said some weren't women, children,
old men; I'd lie too if I claimed these
memories weren't part of my life, but then
shame is natural, wear it, every day
think of bursting from sleep when mortars dropped:
crazy run to a dark hole, damp sandbags.

THEORY

· · · · · · · · · · · · · · · ·

Everybody dug a hole and lived in it
when Division first cleared the land near Cu Chi.
Snipers kept the men low a while, but then tents
went up, then big tents. Later, frames of wood, screen
wire siding, and plywood floors rose under those tents
and that was called a hooch. Time I got there,
base camp was five square miles of hooches, not
a sniper round was fired in daylight, and good posture

was common. What we wanted was a tin roof.
I was there the day we got the tin to do it with,
blistering hot even that morning we stripped off
the old canvas, took hammers and climbed the rafters
to nail down sheets of tin. Drinking beer afterwards,
we were the sweaty survivors, we were the fit.

SMOKE

Base camp smoke was visible fifty klicks
away if you were coming by chopper
up from a three-day pass in Vung Tau or
down past the big mountains near Tay Ninh. Rick
LaTour said the first time he saw it, he
was coming in on the Saigon Express just
at dusk and from the truck it looked pretty.
Rick never said exactly when he first

realized what it was. Explanation
was simple: high water tables meant they
couldn't dig holes; incineration
was logical. Bad duty: to haul those
tubs out from under the outhouses, soak
it with kerosene, let it burn all day.

WORK

· · · · · · · · · · · · · · · · ·

I am a white, Episcopal-raised, almost
college-educated, North American male.
Sergeant Tri, my interpreter, is engrossed
in questioning our detainee, a small,
bad-smelling man in rags who claims to be
a farmer. I am filling in the blanks
of a form, writing down what Sergeant Tri
tells me. This is dull. Suddenly Tri yanks

our detainee to his feet, slaps him twice
across the bridge of his nose. The farmer
whimpers. Tri says the farmer has lied and waits
for orders. Where I grew up my father
waits at the door while my mother finishes
packing his lunch. I must tell Tri what next.

NEW YORK LAUNDRY

Fell in love frequently and had no sense
of correct behavior, was guilty
of imprecise courtship, constructed dense
monologues on individuality,
nature, the body politic, for this
silent laundry girl who always seemed about
to smile, maybe soon would speak, which promise
kept me yammering at her counter without

requitement, Co Tran's humble acolyte.
Buddy of mine set me straight one day, said
Co Tran was famous for being the wife
of the 14th Cav, said those Cav guys praised
the quiet ways of my little Co Tran,
battalion candidate for Short-Time Queen.

BAC HA
· · · · · · · · · · · · · · · · ·

As G-5 put it, Bac Ha hamlet was a good
neighbor in 25th Infantry Division's
eyes. Neighbor was a fact, eyes was a lie, and good
was a joke for a fool. Holes in the fence,
paths to the guard shacks, were for Bac Ha whores,
famous for clap, who maybe last year'd worn white
ao dais and ribboned hats to walk the warm
mornings to school, lessons from French-taught priests.

Division's garbage dump was three acres
fenced off from that hamlet's former front yard.
Black-toothed women, children, former farmers
squatted in the shade all day, smiled at the guards,
watched what the trucks dumped out. Walking nights
out there, you'd be under somebody's rifle sights.

HAIRCUT

Open shop on the strip: Vietnamese barber
standing up is not quite as tall as GI
sitting down, but very serious, scampers
around, snips those scissors, raises them high
over GI's head as if GI had hair
longer than a quarter of an inch to start
with and this was a *salon* in Paris
instead of a shack with no walls and a dirt

floor. At the end he carefully clips hairs
from GI's nose, inserts two small hollow
bamboo sticks in GI's ears, twists them on each
side to ream out the wax, then twangs the sticks. Holds
GI's head, limbers the neck, pops it, scares
GI. Could have died then. 25 p. please.

GEORGE

· · · · · · · · · · · · · · · ·

George Hadley liked a jeep with a two-way
better than most liked their own mothers,
but he was a sweet man, bald, slightly over-
weight to put it politely; liked to cruise
that dusty strip of tin shacks between base
camp and the village, getting himself waved
to and hollered at by the whores, his face
grim as a rock behind cigar and shades.

This Sauna Bath & Massage Parlor opened
up in what looked like it used to be some
farmer's water buffalo slaughterhouse:
two new girls in minis calling, "Come
here, GI!" George decided he'd try it out.
Patted his jeep's fender before he went in.

BEER

Had to send to Saigon for it and what
they sent us was what we got. Sometimes Miller
High Life, Bud, or Black Label, but oh shit!
there was that cheap Australian killer
beer, Swan Lager, God forbid a truckload
of that stuff, it would last for weeks. Better
than no beer, red-haired Leroy always said
when he passed you a can, Leroy getting fatter

by the day sitting behind that bar. Well,
he had a point, because once the truck came back
with not a Goddamn thing but two billion
cans of apricot nectar. We saw Hell
clearly that day. Apricot nectar! Soon
all of us were out there staring at that truck.

R&R

. . . .

Out of Tan Son Nhut flying to Bangkok
on a Pan Am 707 a stewardess
handed out iced-down washcloths, using tongs
to offer them from her tray down to us.
Think about a planeload of soldiers
washing their faces and falling in love,
grunts from the field who'd sweated out their own
deaths for months of nights, administrative

types like me whose days were spent trying
not to drip sweat on reports we'd just typed
up for Captain Kiss My Ass. In Bangkok
I spent three hundred dollars, on women
mostly—don't regret a dime—but what I've kept
is Miss Moore, handing me my cool white cloth.

REVELATION

We spent long days in that hot office hooch
sifting through anybody's report on
anything, tracking down everybody's hunch
that somebody was V.C. or had been one
or was kin to one or maybe they dreamed
they were one once. Our reports were then sent
to the air-conditioned trailer full of agents
who computerized them and sent the machine's

report back to us, a hundred-page printout
that nobody but another machine
could read. One day around four, just before rain
broke, bleary-eyed and T-shirt skinny, Bob Ryan
stopped, face bathed in monsoon light, and
        asked, "You got
any idea how many Nguyen's are in Vietnam?"

WORDS

. . . .

What did those girls say when you walked the strip
of tin shack bars, gewgaw stores, barber shops,
laundries and restaurants, most all of which
had beds in back, those girls who had to get up
in Saigon before dawn to catch their rides to Cu Chi,
packed ten to a Lambretta, chattering, happy
in their own lovely tongue, on the dusty
circus road to work, but then what did they say?

Come here, talk to me, you handsome, GI,
I miss you, I love you too much, you want
short time, go in back, I don't care, I want
your baby, sorry about that, GI,
you number ten. A history away
I translate dumbly what those girls would say.

THEM

Sergeant Dieu, frail Vietnamese man,
once sat down with me, shirtless, on my bunk
and most astonishingly in my opinion
(not his) squeezed a pimple on my back.
My first trip to the field, I saw Vietnamese
infantry troops, loaded with combat gear,
walking the paddy dikes and holding hands.
I was new then. I thought they were queer.

Co Ngoc at the California Laundry
wouldn't say any of our words, but she
explained anyway a Vietnamese treatment
for sore throat: over where it's sore inside
you rub outside until that hurts too. That
way won't work for American pain. I've tried.

TRANSFER

· · · · · · · · · · · · · · ·

Victor Alpha Lima Lima we called
that little bantam section chief we
got stuck with, pretentious SOB
took on that studied wartime disheveled
look, grabbing his hair, whipping his glasses
off to wipe his eyes, talking Vietnamese
to the shoeshine boys, every whip-stitch
giving orders, grabbing the radio mike.

One evening thinking he was clearing
his forty-five, he fired off a round right
beside the Major's hooch, and that same night
Captain Vallyathan's orders were cut to go
some place bad. He came into our hooch, crying,
wanting support. We were short, see. We said no.

SHORT

Because short meant you were going home soon:
on your naked woman whose body was
divided into squares, you'd marked through two
hundred and sixty-five, your style was grab-ass
and beer for breakfast; you were by God
leaving the army and that place for lifers
and any other idiots who liked
it; they could have it, baby, you were gone!

In Oakland to get discharged I talked
to a Corporal Faulkner, asked him was
he kin; he smiled, said no, not to that Faulkner.
Lining up for our last re-up talk, the Corporal
and I laughed. This soft-voiced sergeant spoke, slickest
I'd heard, and after his talk Faulkner up and re-upped.

COUSIN
• • • • • • • • • • • • • • • •
for John H. Kent, Jr., 1919–1982

I grew up staring at the picture of him:
oak leaves on his shoulders, crossed rifles
on his lapels, and down his chest so many medals
the camera lost them. He wore gold-rimmed
glasses, smiled, joked about fear. He told true
stories that were like movies on our front porch:
he'd fought a German hand to hand. The word
courage meant Uncle Jack in World War Two.

Ten years from my war, thirty from his, we
hit a summer visit together; again
the stories came. He remembered names of his men,
little French towns, a line of trees. I could see
his better than mine. He'd known Hemingway!
I tried hard but couldn't find a thing to say.

VERMONT

I'm forty-six. I was twenty-three then.
I'm here with what I've dreamed or remembered.
In the Grand Hotel in Vung Tau one weekend
I spent some time with the most delicate
sixteen-year-old girl who ever delivered
casual heartbreak to a moon-eyed GI.
I am trying to make it balance, but I
can't. Believe me, I've weighed it out:

rising that morning up to the cool air where
the green land moved in its own dream down there,
and I was seeing, the whole flight back to Cu Chi,
a girl turning her elegant face away
after I'd said all I had to say.
This was in Vietnam. Who didn't love me.

II.

ALBUM

for my mother

MUSIC

• • • • • • • • • • • • • • • •

Their white duck trousers, their dark coats, their grave
faces give us out here in the future
to understand such dignity was no
small matter. They surround two demure
women in long dresses, the best piano
players in town. The men hold instruments they've
just started making payments on, their large hands
cradling the horns. Most players of this band,
formally seated here, are carbide men who might
in two hours be shoveling grey dust: trumpet,
trombone, clarinet, tenor saxophone.
The one standing, holding his alto like that,
is my jaunty father, whose music I've known
all my life from this silent black-and-white.

THE FIELD

The breeze stops, the afternoon heat rises,
and she hears his back porch screen door slap shut.
She sits still, lets her mind follow him through
the swinging gate into the field, his shirt
and white flannel pants freshly pressed, his new
racquet held so loosely that it balances
exactly in his hand. Now my father
takes the stile in two steps. And now my mother
turns in the lawn chair, allows herself the sight
of him lifting the racquet as if to
keep it dry. This instant, before he comes
to where she sits under the trees, these two
can choose whatever lives they want, but from
the next it is fixed in shadow and light.

THE HOUSE
· · · · · · · · · · · · · · · · ·

White clapboard of course, but it's of the stained wood
of the stairwell I think first, light slanting
down from the high window at the turn, dust
motes floating for the nap-bound boy standing
with his foot stopped on the first step. He must,
he knows, pass up through shadow to his bed,
but now he's still as light itself. Mother,
he knows you grew up here, too, and Mother,
what's stalled him out here, banister-handed
and knee-bent, is that sight that came to him
from watching that shaft of the afternoon sun
from the high window at the turn. The dim
shape in front of him is a small girl; one
day you stopped here, this way. He's astounded.

TWO FACTS

My mother married when she was fifteen.
Her first child, a girl, lived only minutes.
My father, discussing religion with me,
said he'd "had a hard time" in his twenties.
I think about them. Stopped in reverie
I've held in mind this tableau, this scene:
Faith lost, he sits beside her on the bed.
No child now, she can think only of the dead
child who would have been my older sister.
Though I never saw them so young, I know
how their faces look there, the light falling
in slats into that upstairs bedroom. I know
some of it. But I am afraid of feeling
how much they ache to say *daughter, daughter.*

THE FRONT YARD

The main difference between *yard* and *lawn*
is a yard has crabgrass, dandelions, holes, bumps,
and ruts, while a lawn is smooth. In ours, moles
made sure what we had was a yard. Mother
desired a lawn, though, and called it that. Her
lilacs and forsythia dreamed along
with her, but honeysuckle grew over
our fence, up our porch lattice, and clover—
better for us than for the farmers it bloomed.
Ours was a yard all right. Now I ease
the dark and cold of this northern winter:
I dream a boy with a mason jar for bees,
both honey and bumble, hummingbirds never captured,
and lightning bugs for when it's late in my dark room.

PORCHES

Our front porch faces back toward the road,
the railroad tracks, and the river. A field
of scrub cedars and broomsage holds a path
up which once Crocketts drove their fifty-three
Chrysler, directed by a roadside drunk (half
for fun and half for spite), which episode
showed, though formal callers walk around, our back's
our front—cars come there—and our front's our back,
so that most visitors on a summer day
step up on a damp concrete slab just hosed down,
walk past a cellar door with a hole in it
for the cats, enter the pantry—by now
Mother's face burns—and they all try to fit
in the kitchen and wish they'd come the other way.

GROCERIES IN THE FRONT SEAT

· · · · · · · · · · · · · · · ·

I ask Mother if I can look at the road,
she says yes, and so I open the door
and swing out as far as I can, watching
the blur of our driveway gravel, much more
interesting the closer I get to it. Catching
my belt, Charles asks Mother to stop, in this bored
tone of voice. When she glances back, she screams,
slams on the brakes, switches off the engine, leans
her head on the steering wheel for a while
before she slowly drives the rest of the way
home. She's almost seen her baby crushed.
Charles picks up his comic book, finds his place,
and ignores the looks I give him for having rushed
my contemplation of moving gravel.

INVENTION

Grandmama's little brother, J. C., drove
from Pulaski to speak with my father,
to show him his plans for this new machine
with a series of wheels he thought would gather
energy from these tumbling flaps, hinged
to balance and fold just exactly so.
They talked out by his Hudson, and J. C.'s butt
stuck out when he bent over his papers. "But
J. C.," my father began everything he said.
Until dusk they discussed perpetual motion,
took turns tapping diagrams on the car hood.
Then J. C. drove off, taking his notion
back to Pulaski. For a while my father stood
out there, toeing the gravel, shaking his head.

A HISTORY OF THE PETS

Butch, a black cocker spaniel, collected
stinks, dirt, and open wounds into which our
father poured gentian violet. Did not
come back one morning. A brown and white mutt—
I don't recall its name—was shot by our
mother, beheaded, and pronounced rabid
by health folks who provided all five of us
with fourteen Friday nights of shots. There was
Hooker, half-Persian cat who'd claw your back-
side through the open-backed kitchen chairs and swing
by his hooks till you pulled him loose. Rabbits.
Small possums loose in the house. Short-Circuit,
affectionate cat that walked crooked, that'd been
BB-shot in the head. Goat. Skunk. Some snakes.

DR. ZENO'S LABORATORY

Dr. Zeno's Private Laboratory /
Keep Out / Genius at Work was the sign
Charles hung on the hitherto entirely
uninteresting back room door, which sign
transformed a storage space into nearly
the most desirable territory
I have ever been denied access to,
through which door I heard *Eureka! Presto!*
and *Caramba!* from the place outside where
I stood many minutes hoping he'd let
me in. He did not, though now and then he
stuck his face out, eyebrows raised. Nor did he forget
and let slip the Secret. I'm well past forty;
I still wonder what the hell he did in there.

THE SCHOOL

. . . .

On one side the high school, on the other
grades one through seven, the purple-curtained
auditorium shrank and grew shabbier
each August we came back. Mr. Whitt one year
decided Charles Tomlinson, Slick King, Dwayne
Burchett, Bobby Peaks, and Big Face Cather
could be a basketball team. They practiced
on a rocky, red-dirt court with a basket
and some boards on a post. They drove to games—
always at the other school—in Slick's Ford.
Uniforms were jeans and T-shirts. Big Face
and Bobby played barefoot. They lost by scores
like ten to ninety-three, unaccustomed to such space,
wooden floors, lights, adults calling them names.

THE AIR RIFLE

The double-barreled twelve-gauge that knocked
even our father back a step when he fired it;
the pump-action twenty-gauge he later
gave to me; the pistol (Mother's favorite)
we thought was a Yankee's, its notched hammer
becoming its rear sight when it was cocked;
the damaged Kentucky long rifle;
two over-and-under shotgun rifles;
and a thirty-thirty with a shiny stock.
In the room whose walls held all these weapons,
along with a dull dagger in a sheath
and a dinner horn for calling field hands,
I aimed a toy at my brother's ear, breathed
once, and triggered merely noise with my shot.

CROQUET

This decorous, nineteenth-century
entertainment my Newbern grandmother
and great aunts come down from front porch
    rocking chairs
to play an afternoon hot enough to smother
Methodist ladies who say their prayers
at night but who roquet in quiet fury:
Gran gathers her concentration, pauses,
then lets her red mallet fly forth, causes
her skirt to follow her follow-through, then sweeps
it down and follows her red ball. Two wicked
split shots Aunt Iva fires. Aunt Stella, bones
skewed by childhood polio, makes wicket
after wicket, strikes the post, and in dining room tones
says, "Keep your manners but play for keeps."

ICICLE

I smacked you in the mouth for no good reason
except that the icicle had broken off
so easily and that it felt like a club
in my hand, and so I swung it, the soft
pad of your lower lip sprouting a drop,
then gushing a trail onto the snow even
though we both squeezed the place with our fingers.
I'd give a lot not to be the swinger
of that icicle. I'd like another
morning just like that, cold, windy, and bright
as Russia, your glasses fogging up, your face
turning to me again. I tell you I might
help both our lives by changing that act to this,
by handing you the ice, a gift, my brother.

KITCHEN TABLES

· · · · · · · · · · · · · · · · ·

There were two, small one replacing large one
after Charles and I went to Charlottesville
and left them having meals with only three
to sit down, or sometimes just two because Bill,
with Jim Pope, was out courting catastrophe
in their Dodge or the Popes' Ford, oblivion
turned up high on the radio, Pabst cans
cooling their thighs, both those boys in the trance
of a warm summer night when you're able —
our parents had one daughter who died, three
sons who were always leaving for somewhere —
to race toward some girl's house on county
roads that billow up dust behind you while your
mother and father sit at a small, round table.

SUNDAY DINNER

If the whole length of the white tableclothed
table my grandparents called each other
Old Devil, Battle Ax, Bastard, and Bitch,
if having stopped smoking for Lent, Mother
was in a pout, if New Deal politics
had my father telling us how much he loathed
Roosevelt, if Grandma Lawson's notion
that we boys needed a dose of worm potion
had Charles trying hard not to look amused
and Bill whining for dessert even though
he hadn't finished his beets, if all this
and Uncle Lawrence's thick White Owl smoke,
Aunt Elrica's hoots, and Inez's craziness
weren't my one truth, I'd ask to be excused.

CODA

Sons grown and gone, they adopt a mutt
that comes, stays ten years, and learns their ways.
On slow walks that good dog leads my parents
a hundred yards out the gravel driveway
until a gunshot rips through one day's silence.
My mother and father break into a trot,
though they are old now, too old to run like
this to the curve of the road and the sight
of fat old Daisy's neck a bloody spout,
one spent shell a step away, smoke still spooling,
the backs of two running boys, the one not
carrying the gun looking back and laughing.
They are not strong enough to lift the weight
of their dog. They turn back to the empty house.

Through the hundreds of miles between my house
and theirs, my daughters, my wife, and I
take turns talking with my parents in our
twice-a-month phone call. In our talk we try
to pretend it won't be long before our
visit next summer. I hardly hear how
their words sound; I've lost them and they've lost me,
this is just habit, blood, and memory.
They pause, then they tell us about Daisy,
how she must have walked right up to those boys
before they shot her down . . . And yes, I am
seeing just how it was. My mother's voice
breaks. I am with you, I want to tell them,
but I manage to say only that I see.

III.

STOPPING
BY HOME

. . . .

Five times since July my father
has been hospitalized. He's home
today, sitting up at his desk
in bathrobe, pajamas, slippers.
I am embarrassed, I want him
fat again, in khakis that smell
like sweat, cigarette smoke, carbide,

ignoring me because he'd rather
work the crossword puzzle, alone
or pretending to be, than risk
in those minutes before supper
finding out what meanness I'd been
up to. He's thin now. And pale.
Waiting to hear what's on my mind.

. . . .

In the summer in the hospital
he sat on the bed's edge clutching
that Formica table they crank up
and put your food tray on. He coughed
up white mucus, took oxygen
from a thin green tube, couldn't sleep,
couldn't lie back and breathe. He

and my mother thought it was all
finished the day he got medicine
to make him relax, make him sleep,
then couldn't sit up because he'd lost
his strength but couldn't breathe lying
back. They rang for the nurse, but he
passed through something you couldn't see.

. . . .

They say his hair turned white. It's true,
it's grayer than it was, almost
white. He can't read much now, has no
power of concentration, mind
strays. Today he talks about friends
who've died, relatives long gone.
In a photograph he points out

which ones are dead now. "But you
and Lester Waller and Tom Pope
and George Schreiber and James Payne—so
many still alive," I remind
him. He seems not to hear and bends
to put the picture away. "Some
still around," he says. "Yes, no doubt."

. . . .

My mother wants us to talk. This
is what she always wants, her sons
sitting around with their dad, talk
being evidence of love, she
thinks. My evenings home from school,
the army, New York, or Vermont,
she'd leave the room for us to do it.

We always argued politics.
Didn't intend to, but reasons
came to us. Once he said I ought
to go to Russia and see
how what I'd just said was pure bull,
and I walked out. Words are too hard
for us now. We'll just have to sit.

. . . .

Their lives in that house before he got too sick must have been
so filled with silence that even when a truck would pass
on the highway down the hill they would listen. Those
clear sunny days of May and June she sat with him
on the front porch where sometimes the soft wind
rustled in that hack-berry that's grown
so high now. I hold an infant

recollection of the sun
warming the three of us,
their holding me so
close between them
I knew then
what home
meant.

So
if I
care so much
about them I
have to sit up here
a thousand miles away
and write myself back home, why

not look for a job down there, try
to find some town close enough to say,
"I'm going to see them," drive over there
and walk in the door and not even surprise
them, sit down with them and talk, maybe stay for lunch,
say an easy good-bye and leave without feeling like
I betrayed them, and I will never find my way back home.

. . . .

Night comes down, the winter sky
momentarily ecstatic,
then stunned, bruised, ruined with pain, dark . . .
Coal on the fire, our old habits
keep us still, without lights, sitting
until the study's bay window
yields maybe one moving tree branch.

Then Mother rises, breathes a sigh
for all three of us when she flicks
on the overhead light. The dog barks
lightly in its sleep. We blink. It's
not late. His fingers shake setting
his watch. Before us are the slow
hours, each breath he takes a chance.

. . . .

At six we move from the study
to the living room for the news,
the weather report our excuse.
The man draws snow over the whole
Northeast, freely uses the word
blizzard, and I stand up before
he's finished and say I think I

better keep driving north, maybe
I can beat that storm. "But Son, you
just got here." Mother's hurt. He's used
to my skedaddling ways, and so
makes himself grin, offers his hand
for me to shake and at the door
we say our word for love. Good-bye.

• • • • • • • • • • • • • • • • •

I scuttle out into the dark
and drive three hundred miles north, numb,
knowing that I hurt but not able
to register it, a busted
speedometer on a car that
hurtles forward. In the morning
I get what's coming to me. Snow

starts in Pennsylvania, slick
stuff on those mountains south of Scranton,
the interstate a long white table
of ice, everything blasted
white. Wind and drifts in those high flat
stretches near nowhere. Endless dream
of losing control, moving through snow.

• • • • • • • • • • • • • • • • •

Tell me whose parents don't get old.
Your father's sick, and you can't stand
to be around him and help him
die or get well, whichever it
turns out he's going to do. Well,
son, you deserve to drive through snow,
wind and freezing cold, past Hometown,

Port Jervis, Newburgh, Kingston. No
decent motel would have you, can't
stop, can't give your old man an arm
to help him walk into the next
room. Albany says go to hell,
keep driving, boy, get your ass home
where you've got children of your own.

IV.

. . . .

THINGS I KNOW, THINGS I DON'T

. . . .

Virginia in early October
is a soft countryside, color not yet
in the trees but the leaves' green going pale,
the sunlight's angle sharp, the birds about
to move. Those cool mornings you catch a whiff
of woodsmoke, evenings you feel a chill
ring the air like a high, soft-blown flute note.
That season of my father's death was not
wrong, not wrong at all. If he had been well
that day he might have taken a walk with
Mother, one of their short strolls. Early that
morning there'd been heavy fog that was all
gone by nine. He'd have liked how that sun felt
on his shoulders. He'd have liked that weather.

. . . .

Wytheville Hospital, February 1985

To help his cracked rib heal, he was supposed
to wear a rib brace with a Velcro seam.
Charles and I hadn't seen him so confused

(though one night at home he'd made Charles let
      him lean
on him while he urinated from his upstairs
bedroom window, thanked Charles nicely when
      the stream

ended, then went back to bed). Anyway, there
we'd driven a thousand miles to his bedside
and our assignment was to make him wear

this corset he'd want loose and then decide
it wasn't tight enough, and he got the word
Velcro on his mind, would say it every five

seconds, "Get this Velcro fixed, Dave," or weird
things like, "I gotta go to Velcro now."
About the sixty-seventh time I'd heard

"Fix the Velcro, Dave," I gave him a scowl
and told him I guessed he could live with it
the way it was. It was late, I was out

of patience, having been his good servant
all afternoon. (Charles would take the morning
shift.) Hallway noise made the room seem quiet,

and the blank, beige wall was occupying
his attention like a text he was about
to be quizzed on. But then he was eyeing

me in that sideways way of his, and out
of the corner of his mouth, he said, "If
I were a little stronger, I'd kick your butt."

I wish I could say I stuffed a handkerchief
in my mouth, but for most of my life we'd
been arguing. "You could fix it yourself,

if you were a little stronger," I said,
and he said yes, he guessed that was the truth.
Not much dialogue after that. He faded

back to talking with dead Uncle Jack, with
men who'd worked for him at the carbide plant.
He called me Charles or Bill, let loose a hoot

now and then, "Velcro, Velcro!" or "I want,
the urinal!" or once just "Weewee, weewee!"
and I'd help him with that, though it wasn't

ever more than a drop or two. Easy,
after a while, waiting on him that way,
when I had dreaded it so intensely

I thought I'd freeze up if I had to stay
with him an hour by myself. That night
driving his car out on the interstate

I imagined Mother driving him there right
after he'd taken the fall that broke his rib.
She'd just finished lecturing him about

not doing enough for himself, when he slipped
trying to stand up and fell against a chair
right in front of her eyes. Ashamed, mad, scared,

she must have known more then about despair
than I'd learn in my lifetime. We'd lost count
of his trips to the hospital that year

and the year before. Almost always he got
worse, they sent him home hinting that he'd die
soon, but then somehow he'd improve and astound

us all. Without seeming to try, he survived.
It wasn't the man's will to live; it was
his fear of dying, I thought, but then I'd

always judged him harshly. Next morning Charles
and Mother questioned me all through breakfast.
I told about the Velcro, but as far as

I was concerned, the butt-kicking lambaste
and what I'd said were my business. Charles said
when he'd teased him yesterday, Dad had asked

him to please stop the cutting up. "Ah, God,
Charles," he'd groaned, "you have cut up so damn much!"
The way we laughed then made it seem not so bad,

though of course things were terrible, he in such
relentless misery, Mother depressed
and exhausted, Charles and I good for just

a few days of help, when it was endless:
for years he was going to be running
up to death and out over the abyss

like the Roadrunner coyote, cunning
in spite of himself, clawing his way back
to life after we'd all given up on him.

We didn't then, at breakfast, or in fact
ever, acknowledge what was obvious:
if he got better, another attack

would come in a few months, and they got worse
each time. If he got better, we had it all
to go through again. "And what about us!"

I might have yelped, but I wanted my small
soul out of sight. What I meant was Me! What
about Me? I hated the hospital,

hated my father's dying the way I'd hate
to sit still, listening to someone's soft,
constant weeping, someone I couldn't

help at all. That morning I read half
of Susan Cheever's *Home Before Dark,* her
memoir of her troubled father enough

to make me forget mine. It was Cheever
I thought about that afternoon, driving
back to the hospital to take my turn

again. When I walked in, Charles was smiling
as if our sleeping father had told a joke
he wanted to tell me, he was spinning

me around to the door, pushing me back
into the hallway. We leaned on the wall.
"Weewee! Weewee!" he whispered in a croak,

but you laugh softly in a hospital
if you laugh at all. When Charles left, I walked
back in and sat down. My father was still

asleep; his breathing pulled his neck cords taut,
then let them loose. I had to will myself
not to sit and gape while his body fought

to keep the life in him. I'd think, what if
this is his last breath, what if he dies now,
this instant, while I'm watching. Then he'd shift

a leg or cough or rub his nose, and I'd know
he was miles from death and call myself a fool.
John Cheever was gravely ill but somehow

managing to keep himself witty, cool,
decorous, and brave, snubbing his cancer,
bearing his pain. Achieving a final

dignity seemed to be Cheever's answer
to his years of drunken ignominy.
My father had to wear adult Pampers,

had to be spoon-fed, his exemplary
sober lifetime having earned him the right
to have his sons treat him like a baby.

I looked up and saw his face in the light,
looking right at me but with his eyes glazed.
I doubted he knew me. In this polite

voice he said, "Dave," and swallowed and said,
"I want to go home." I said, "Well, I know
you do." He held my eye, and time passed

like a stopped train. "To Ivanhoe,"
he said as if I didn't know that sorry
town where we'd all grown up, that cruel joke

of a town so poor, so mean, and so ugly
that all you had to do was say the name
in Wytheville and somebody would swear he

almost got killed there one night. But right then
I knew what he had in mind, long summer
days, afternoons turning cool, croquet games

until full dark. "Ivanhoe," he murmured,
"Ivanhoe, sweet Ivanhoe." He was quiet
then, holding it in his mind; then he stirred

his legs, threshed his arms, asked me Goddamnit
what was I waiting for, go get the car
and pull it up to the door—he pointed

toward the hallway—he'd meet me right there.
I explained about how when he got well
we'd take him home, we'd take him anywhere

he wanted to go, we'd take him—"Ah hell,
Son," he said. Then it was as if he hung
up the phone on me and let himself fall

into confusion and delirium.
He picked at the sheets and spoke to a man
who had apparently emerged from the ceiling,

asking my father for money. I can
take just so much craziness. I read hard:
Cheever's family gathered around him;

the minister had trouble in the dark
bedroom reading the last rites, ". . . thy servant,
John." They said the Lord's Prayer, then John's heart

stopped. "It was so fast, it was so fast," wrote
Susan. I looked up and watched my father's slow
demented gaze sweep the room, saw him point

toward that place in the ceiling as though
he'd just driven away his enemy.
He'd lost so much weight that he seemed more bone

than flesh . . . Here was some old geek claiming he
was the same man who'd showed me how to blow
soap bubbles in the bathtub, how to read

music, how to drive a car, showed me how
trying to be honest, work hard and raise
a family was one way you could go

to bed at night and get some sleep. Here was
this babbling monster who'd stolen the life
my father made with thirty thousand days

of labor and decency. Now here it
pointed to the light, it made a quick stab,
it lurched in its bed and swung its arm as if

battling something invisible. "Want," it said.
Would it ever stop Goddamn wanting? "On,"
it moaned. "No!" I rasped at it. I was mad

enough to walk out. "You need a light on
to read," my father said. "Turn it on, Son."

. . . .

Harmonicas kept turning up in desk drawers,
filing cabinets, and attic boxes—
weathered rectangular boxes with pictures
of German marching bands on the lids, inside

they were shining metal with a brassy smell.
Exploring his stuff, my brothers and I
dug them out of places he'd stashed them.
Sometimes he'd take an interest in one

that hadn't made a sound for twenty years.
This would be while he sat at his desk
with a boy at each elbow, another at his knee.
He'd cup the harmonica in both hands and blow

a few notes. Always he stopped and looked
away from us boys there waiting for him
to go on with *The Black Hawk Waltz, Little
Redwing,* or *She'll Be Coming 'Round the Mountain.*

. . . .

He hit me once
                lightly
when I was cutting up in the bathtub
with one of my brothers. I do not
remember the hit.
                I remember
splashing the warm water,
the white tub all around,
him sitting above it,
wiping off his glasses,
not laughing
anymore.

• • • • • • • • • • • • • • • • •

To court my mother he walked over to her house to play tennis with her and my Aunt Murrell. There must have been a fourth, but I don't know who that was. It must have started when she was around thirteen, when he'd recovered from rheumatic fever and instead of going back to Emory & Henry to finish a degree in physics he'd gone to work for his father at the sand plant mostly because Grandmama couldn't stand the idea of his going away and getting sick again. His features were delicate; his tennis whites set off his skin, sun-darkened that summer from their daily games; he was tall and thin and had good manners; he played all sorts of musical instruments; he read magazines and books Mother had never heard of; and on the tennis court, he was both a gentleman and a fine athlete. When it got dark I'm sure she had to go inside, but twilights last hundreds of years up there where she lived, and the fireflies come out in that first cool air that prickles the skin of your arm. When old full dark came slowly down, he said, "Your white dress is holding all the light." Her older sister walked indoors, and that faceless fourth rode a rickety old bike out the driveway and out of their memories forever, but still they stood there talking about shooting stars. The miracle of it is that they waited two more years before marrying. Whenever they told us about their tennis, they made it clear they both played well.

• • • • • • • • • • • • • • • •

"Duck-footed,"
Monkey said,
"is how you
Huddles walk,"
the occasion
for Monkey's
observation
being his and my
walking from
the barn to
somewhere and
seeing Charles
walking from
somewhere else
toward the barn,
when Monkey,
who'd started
school with our
father but hadn't
gotten further
than about fifth
grade when he
quit, Monkey
who in most
circumstances
was kindness
incarnate, but
who suffered
the failing
of the truly
ignorant, the
inability to
see other than
accurately, said,
"Look at that boy
walk, walks just
like your daddy,"
and I, whose
IQ was already
several points
higher than his
even though my

head came to
just about his
belt, I who
would attend
fourteen more
years of school
than he and who
had already
taken to spending
as many hours
every day staring
into a mirror
as Monkey did
praying and he
prayed a lot, I who
had this vision
of myself as an
amalgamation
of a cowboy movie
star, a Cleveland
Indians pitcher
and a benign
millionaire,
asked him, "How's
that, Monkey?"
and he said,
"Duck-footed,
honey, don't you
know all you
Huddles walk
that way?" and I
said, "I don't,"
and he glanced
at me and said,
"That's just because
you're making your
feet stay straight,"
then looked at me
again and laughed
and went on to say,
"Honey, it's nothing
to be ashamed of.
All you Huddles
walk kind of
duck-footed."

• • • • • • • • • • • • • • • • • •

Christmas vacation of 1960, my first year at the
University of Virginia we were up late talking
and I asked my father (because my best friend
from the dorm had confided in me that he
was one) what he knew about homosexuals,
and my father said nothing, said he didn't
know a thing, and do you know what
he did? (This will tell you everything
you need to know about the time and
the place I grew up in and the kind
of family we were.) My father
got out the dictionary
and looked
that word
up.

● ● ● ● ● ● ● ● ● ● ● ● ● ● ● ● ●

Because you see books was what
they put their faith in,
my father and my grandfather,
what they turned to when

they hit something they didn't
know about and wanted to,
or any kind of problem, like how
you dug postholes, how you

stored apples, or covered a cistern.
My grandfather taught
himself veterinary medicine,
chemistry (he also bought

all the stuff you needed
to practice these things—tools,
equipment, drugs, machinery,
chemicals, cabinets, and scales),

learned watch repairing,
welding, farming, plumbing, carpentry,
bee- and orchard-keeping, oil painting.
That man would try

anything, and everything meant
a set of books, his proudest
possession the five shelves
of volumes that meant he'd finished

the International Correspondence School
course of instruction
in civil engineering. His income
matched the multiplication

of his interests for a while,
and his house was headquarters
of Charlie Huddle's Empire,
my father his somewhat smarter

but less imaginative assistant.
Nowadays we know the history
of empires. My grandfather lived
to see his machinery

auctioned off, but even then
he and my father pored over
books, calculating what to hold
on to, hoping to discover

the key to preserving what
they'd built up. If charts
existed, they'd probably show
1950 as my grandfather's

last good year, though the downward
curve would be a slow slide.
And though Hiroshima and Nagasaki
were on the opposite side

of their globe, he and my father
understood the men who made
the bomb, men of science, men
who solved problems, who read

books and figured out how
to stop a war. The family line
was that Roosevelt and the New
Deal caused the decline

in our fortune. So when I moved
to New York City to attend
Columbia and once wrote out
for my father a passage I found

in *The New York Times Book Review*,
something Buckminster Fuller
said about work being one
of the silliest human activities ever

invented, I was carrying out a tradition
of digging wisdom out
of books and sharing it with my kin.
When he sent back a quote

from William Henry Hudson that said
(and here I must paraphrase
from memory), "Sir, I cannot help
but recognize what is false

when I directly encounter it,"
my ears burned, but I could see
him checking through our bookshelves
for Hudson, William Henry,

and hoping he could find those words
he only dimly remembered.
And years after Grandad's death,
when his house had to be emptied,

my father and brothers and I worked
for days cataloging all
those books we didn't want sold
for nothing: one would call

out the author, the title,
and the publisher; another would
type it up; and another would put
them in stacks that stood

wall to wall in the library,
the parlor and the hallway.
Even though my father just sat
and told us what to do that day,

he was there working with us,
helping solve the problem
of what to do with Grandad's library.
Emphysema weakened him

later so that he hardly left his bed,
though he lived long enough
to see the manuals, texts,
medical books, the most valuable stuff

(we'd all thought) sold for almost nothing.
We couldn't even give away
that correspondence school course
in civil engineering.

. . . .

The phone
woke her and she knew
instantly, Mother said. A nurse said he
seemed to be—there is
no word

that suits
what was happening
to him in those early morning hours,
and I don't know what
they said

really—
seemed to be *dying*
I will say here instead of the *going*
that first came to mind,
they said

he was
dying—my mother
heard that word singing through the telephone
and it must have been
the sound

she'd heard
whispered in her dreams.
She got up quickly, dressed, made herself think
of everything,
stepped out

and turned
to lock the door when
she realized it wasn't just dark out
there, there was a fog
so thick

the end
of the lighted porch
was invisible to her. But she kept
going, she walked
on out

toward
the garage, her hand
outstretched, touching nothing, the light behind
her diminished now,
she took

two more
steps, and the planet
dropped away from her, she couldn't even
see her feet. *I am,*
she thought,

*going
to the hospital
to be with my husband who is dying.*
She took one more step
and closed

her eyes,
and it was the same
darkness either way, eyes closed, eyes open.
She thought it harder
this time:

*I am
going . . .* She turned back,
and in four steps she could see the porch light.
She went in and made
coffee

and sat
down at the table
with the empty cup in front of her, she
lost track of time, she
sat there,

and I
was asleep beside
my wife here in Vermont, Charles was asleep
in Rhode Island, Bill
asleep

out west,
all the grandchildren
sleeping, the ninety-seven-year-old mother
in the nursing home
asleep.

But he
was not alone, there
were nurses, Doctor Roda walked up there
to the hospital
knowing

a man
he'd kept alive was
going to—did those people have the right
word, did they say he's
going

to die?
Do I know if they'd
say that? I have to see them there beside
his bed, three of them,
watching

him breathe,
taking his pulse, then
catching each other's eyes when there was no
more breath, no more pulse,
no more

life.
What
words were spoken then,
when they had to turn away from what they
had witnessed? I want
their words

to be
common: *Do you want
some coffee? Is it still foggy out there?*
even *I've got to
take a*

piss. I
want them to be who
they are, my mother in the car later
making her way there
to be

who she
is, my brothers, my
children, my nieces and nephews, even
old deaf Grandmama,
I want

no one
ever again like
Mother to have to grope out into that
complete darkness
where it

didn't
matter if she was
alive or dead, for that moment she was
not anywhere and did not
matter.

He was.
I say my father was
here. I say he lived thousands of strong days.
I know he got sick. My
father

died. I
can say that, can walk
from home to work, can touch my daughter's hair,
can say anything
I want.